He Said,
"Peace Be Still"

Anthony Liguori, Jr.

PublishAmerica
Baltimore

First printing

ISBN: 1-4137-9605-2
PUBLISHED BY PUBLISHAMERICA, LLLP
www.publishamerica.com
Baltimore

Printed in the United States of America

DEDICATION

This book is dedicated with love to my wife, Jeannette. Without her love, support and guidance this book and my many other accomplishments would not have been possible. I love you more than life itself. To my "sons of thunder," Christian and Joshua, your madcap adventures never cease to put a smile on my face and bring joy to my heart.

TABLE OF CONTENTS

He Said, "Peace Be Still"

Introduction

Is there life after death? Have you ever asked yourself that question before? Be truthful now, I'm sure we all have at one time or another. No matter how strong our faith or religious beliefs, we are afraid of the unknown. I can tell you first hand that I certainly had my doubts and fears about dying and life after death. By the grace of God, the extraordinary story I am about to tell you has taken away all my doubts and fears. What lies ahead is a true story of a beautiful journey so profound that it has changed my life forever. The events that I'm going to tell you about have been vividly burned into my mind's eye. This is a story of hope and transformation that healed my wounded and troubled soul, giving me the strength and courage to go on. My prayer is that the lives of all who read this story will be touched by the love and light of Jesus in the same way He has graciously touched my life.

As a child I always had a special attraction to Jesus. Though at the time, I didn't understand why. Whenever I saw a picture or statue of Jesus, it made me feel good. While I was growing up, my parents raised me in the Catholic faith. However, religion wasn't the main focus in our family's life. Even though my parents took my brother, sister and I to church and Sunday school, you wouldn't exactly call us a very religious family. We seemed to go through the motions just like a lot of other "Christian" families.

I recall having my first real spiritual experience one day when I was eight years old, which took place during my First Holy Communion. I can remember it like yesterday. My eyes were staring in awe at the large wooden crucifix behind the altar. I had been transfixed looking at the body of Jesus on the cross. I began to experience this warm feeling coming over my body. Then suddenly as I was sitting in my pew, I thought I heard the voice of God talking to me, asking me to follow him. Even though I was very young, I knew that one day God would have something special planned for me. From that day on the image of Jesus hanging upon the cross began to leave a lasting impression on me. I now felt myself strangely attached to this man called Jesus. I didn't really know him, yet I felt very close to him. Looking back I sometimes wonder if I could have missed his calling.

Until recently, I thought that eight years old was much too young to make any kind of rational decision about a calling from God. Then one day when I was speaking with my pastor, Father Jim, he told me that coincidently he had also experienced his first calling from God at the age of eight. Being young and a little scared, I just hadn't understood the sign.

As the years went by, I played down my communion experience, thinking I had just gotten caught up in my "special day." I began to convince myself that I had probably let my emotions and imagination run wild, yet I still had this strange feeling to find out more about Jesus. Back in the sixties and seventies, the channel seven 4:30 movie would always show biblical movies during Easter week. Now I know what you're thinking: The 4:30 movie? This guy is really showing his age. They screened such classics as *King of Kings*, *Ben Hur* and *The Greatest Story Ever Told*, all depicting the life of Jesus. And all, may I add, with far too many commercial breaks. I began watching these movies every year (remember, this was before videos kids) and they soon became my favorites. At the time it seemed to be a great way to learn more about Jesus. This was kind of like the way I did my book reports in school. I would watch the movie instead of reading the book. In this case, "The Good Book."

I also recall seeing a movie called *The Shoes of the Fisherman* starring Anthony Quinn as the Pope. I really liked that movie a lot. I thought Anthony Quinn was cool and I liked his portrayal of the Pope. I was convinced that when I grew up, I would one day be the Pope. Most little boys want to be a policeman or a fireman like their dads. But not me, it was the Pope or nothing. Well, we all know that never happened to say the least! I loved watching those movies and still do today, but at the time I wasn't grasping the whole picture.

As I was reaching adulthood, I still was not a very religious person though I desired to be one. I often felt like I just didn't fit in anywhere. I seemed to be always searching for something, trying to fill a void in my life. I was about to find out shortly just what it was that I was searching for.

Chapter One

Looks Can Be Deceiving

My story begins on August 7, 1960. I was born in Hackensack Hospital in Hackensack, New Jersey. I was the second of three children born to my mother, Florence, and my father, Anthony. We lived in a small apartment in Hackensack.

At age three my family moved us to Saddle Brook, New Jersey, where I attended grade school and high school. Saddle Brook was a nice middle-class town to grow up in during the 1960s. The decade of the '60s for me was a happy and simple time of *Flintstone* pajamas, playing cowboys and Indians, and coming home when the streetlight turned on. I loved music, sports and had a lot of friends. In fact, I still keep in touch with several of my friends from the old neighborhood.

My father was an only child, so my grandparents spent a lot of time with my family. My grandfather was an exceptionally kind and gentle man, who was loved by all of his family and friends. He would always buy my brother, sister and I all the latest toys, games, bicycles and clothes. We had a very nice home. On the outside we looked like the perfect family with the white picket fence. However, looks can be deceiving. My father had a quick and violent temper. His motto was, "Hit first and ask questions later." Many nights I would lie awake listening to my parents argue in the other room. It seemed as if they fought constantly, and many times things would get way out of hand. My mother tried her best to give us a stable home life, but it became apparent that she was fighting a losing battle. I remember always being scared and praying to God for help! My parents did a great job of hiding all of this from most of our family and friends. I, too, did my best to try and hide this dysfunctional life I was living at home.

I entered Saddle Brook High School in the fall of 1974 at age 14. Once again, I found it easy to make friends. I was popular with my classmates, and to my surprise, I was elected class president. In Spanish class during my junior year, I met my childhood sweetheart and future wife, Jeannette. I was failing Spanish big time and Jeannette was trying her hardest to help me pass. Fate would have it that we both dropped Spanish class and became an "item." Till this day neither one of us can speak Spanish, but I'm proud to say that we are still happily married.

In order to cope with my family life, I kept myself very busy with outside activities. I became the all-star running back for our varsity high school football team, the Saddle Brook Falcons. Football was my passion, second only to my love of music. I began to focus my entire life on sports and music. As far back as I can remember, I was always singing. In fact, my mother mentions in my baby book that I loved to sing "Cowboy" songs as a young child. One of my all-time favorite songs was titled, "The Rebel, Johnny Yuma." This was the opening song for a cowboy western show with the same title and was sung by Johnny Cash. I loved that show, and every morning I would dress like "Johnny Yuma" with my rebel hat and cap gun and listen to that song.

During high school, most of my friends were listening to The Who or Led Zeppelin. However, I was a huge Elvis Presley fan and made no apologies for it. Elvis and his music would one day become a major influence on my musical career. I formed my first rock band and also joined the Saddle Brook High School Choir. Our high school had an excellent choir director named Charles Broadhurst. Mr. B, as we called him, would become one of my early role models. I credit him for helping to shape who and what I would become in later years. He helped me to grow in my love and appreciation for music. Mr. B was a kind and wonderful man who possessed great Christian moral values. We remained close friends and he continued to lend moral support and guidance throughout my entire music career until his untimely death in 2004. The day Mr. Broadhurst passed was one of the saddest days of my life.

My family life at home did not get any better. In fact things got a lot worse. It was at this time when I pretty much stopped going to church altogether. My grades began to slip and I began to totally focus my life on art and music. My father was a good artist, and I inherited this talent naturally. I graduated high school in 1978 and set my eyes on an art career, hoping to graduate from a top New York art school. Due to circumstances out of my control, I was not able to follow the path I had chosen.

Chapter Two

Hellish Nightmare

As I was reaching adulthood, my life began to rapidly change. I was out of high school and had to settle for a community college. Although it was not my school of choice, I was making the best of my situation. I realized the importance of a good education and that it would be a mistake to quit. Unfortunately, without the financial support of my parents, I was forced to quit.

At the same time I was becoming estranged from most of my friends I'd had since childhood. They were beginning to hang out with a "bad" crowd, one from which I was struggling to stay away. I didn't want any part of the drug and alcohol scene. Yet without my friends, I began to feel very lonely. Then to complicate matters even more, my home life was turning into a child's worst nightmare. My parents' marriage, which had been deteriorating for years, was heading towards a bitter divorce.

Their strained relationship had finally taken its toll on the entire family. I felt like I had to "walk on eggshells" every day of my life, and that is not a healthy way to live.

I love both of my parents and I don't hold anything against either one. At the time, though, I was very angry and scared and it seemed like my world was falling apart. I was not prepared to deal with these harsh realities of life. All at once my life was becoming real complicated, and I just wasn't mature enough to handle it. The combination of all these things made me very depressed, and I felt like I had nowhere to turn. I was filled with self-pity and just didn't care anymore. It's sad to admit, but I was beginning to lose the will to live. I began to focus my entire life on a music career and "making it big." But the Lord had something else planned for me.

One day I began to experience severe pain in my abdomen. At first I didn't tell anyone. I tried to deal with it myself and hoped the pain would go away. This went on for a few weeks until finally I had to be rushed to the hospital. During my first exam, the doctor on call diagnosed me with acute gastritis, better known as gas pains. I was given antacid tablets and released from the emergency room. As I was leaving the hospital, a nurse made a remark under her breath saying, "This kid will be back." She was right. The next day I was rushed back to the hospital in the backseat of my father's Buick in a fetal position. The five-minute ride to the hospital seemed like it took hours. Every bump the car hit in the road made me scream out in agony. This time the doctor on call knew there was something severely wrong with me and had to perform emergency exploratory surgery.

While they were wheeling me into the OR, the pain was getting so bad, I remember saying to myself, "Dying would be better than being in this much pain," and I really meant it. My body was trembling and I was in excruciating pain. I began to break out in a cold sweat. The last thing I remember was the anesthesiologist putting the mask on my face, telling me to count back from one hundred, and at ninety-eight, I was out cold.

I woke up hours later in the middle of the night in the intensive care unit in Hackensack Hospital. I remember the room being pitch dark and my first instinct was to sit up. As I moved my body forward, I felt a severe pain in my abdomen and I collapsed back onto the bed. At this time I didn't realize the severity of my condition.

As in lay in pain, I looked around the room and began to see some very strange things. The room seemed to be in a whirlwind filled with pale, ghost-like apparitions flying all around me. I was terrified. My first thought was that I must have died and gone to hell. I thought Satin must have easily won possession of my soul because of the weak and depressed state I was in. I felt like I deserved to be there to suffer in my shame and sorrow. When you are in such a weak physical and mental condition, that is when the devil tries to take control. Then suddenly, I felt someone gently take hold of my hand. I looked to the left of my bed and thought that it was a nurse in her white uniform, comforting me. However, as I looked at her face, I realized that the nurse was my great aunt Rose O'Riley. Aunt Rose was my grandfather's sister, who had been deceased for many years. She was such a beautiful woman who had always shown so much love and kindness to all our family. My aunt didn't say a word; she just smiled at me, and I began to feel safe in the midst of this hellish "nightmare." As I reflect, I find it fitting that Aunt Rose would be the angel "sent" to comfort me and lead me back from the dark side. I suddenly fell back into a deep, deep sleep.

I woke up in the hospital a day or so after my surgery hooked up to all kinds of tubes and machines. I was dazed and confused and wasn't quite sure what had happened to me. I later found out that my omentum, a protective flap that covers the vital organs, had twisted and cut off the blood flow to the lower portion and had to be partially removed. Gangrene had already set in and was poisoning my body. For several days they had to pump the toxic poison from my body. A nurse told me that there was only one other case like this in the history of Hackensack Hospital at the time. She also told me I was lucky I survived.

I was released from the hospital about a week later and went home to recover. After a few days home, I began to recall the strange event that had occurred while I was in ICU. I wondered if it had just been a bad dream or the side effects of the anesthesia that had caused me to see these awful things. However, I thought it seemed too real. I wasn't quite sure what to think.

After being home a week or so, I seemed to fall back into that same old deep depression. The situation at home with my parents was getting worse than ever, and I just didn't know where to turn. One night I remember feeling so depressed that I wished my life would end. Thoughts of how I could take my own life began to creep into my head. I began to feel strangely excited and almost happy thinking of ways to bring my life to an abrupt end. Once again, the evil power of Satan was trying to take advantage of a weak and depressed soul. I could clearly hear the devil's voice telling me how easy it would be to take my own life and how my pain and suffering would soon be over. As I look back, it's scary to think how close I actually came to taking my own life. I still get cold chills just thinking about it. As the darkness of night crept in on me, I became extremely terrified and I pulled the bed covers up close to my face. I can remember lying in my bed, trembling with my heart beating out of control. In my head, I was crying out, "God, please take me, I just don't want to live!" I was hysterically crying and so physically drained that I fell into the deepest, darkest sleep I have ever felt in my life.

Chapter Three

Peaceful Journey

As my body lay there almost lifeless, I began to feel dizzy and my soul started to lift out of my body. For lack of any other term I was about to have what people call a "near death" or "out-of-body" experience. The only explanation I can give for leaving my body is that I had sunk so low that I had actually willed myself to die. My soul floated up above my bed, through the ceiling and into a dark tunnel. I could see a bright light at the far end, and my body seemed to be speeding towards the light. As I looked on each side of the tunnel, I saw ghostly, tormented souls screaming in the darkness. They were moving past me at a rapid pace in the opposite direction, away from the light. They were similar to the apparitions I had recently seen in the intensive care unit. I was scared and unsure where I was headed. Finally I reached the end of the tunnel and emerged on the other side. As soon as I arrived, I knew I was in a "good" place.

I was standing in a field of emerald green grass. I remember thinking, "I've never seen grass so green and beautiful." As I looked around, this green field stretched to the left and right of me as far as the eye could see. Then I noticed that directly in front of me there were large green hedge bushes. They seemed to be about twelve feet high and stretched once again to the right and left as far as the eye could see. The hedge was thick and I was unable to see through it. It seemed to me that the hedge was some kind of wall guarding a sacred place. All at once I began to feel a dizzy weightlessness about me. My body began to rise up into the air, lifting me over this wall of hedges.

I gently landed on the other side of this "wall." As I steadied myself, I looked up and could not believe what I was seeing. I was in a place so beautiful words could not describe it. At this point I knew that I could be nowhere else but in heaven. Everything was so vibrant and peaceful, and I felt strangely at home. Once again I noticed that the grass was so green it almost looked like velvet. There were flowers and trees everywhere. It was like a huge botanical garden a billion times more beautiful than any I have seem in my life. As I looked at the flowers, they seemed to have a colored light coming from within them that glowed. Every flower and tree had a beautiful musical tone coming out of it. The music was so beautiful, however, unlike any I'd ever heard before. All the plant life seemed to be dancing in time to the music. I remember seeing colors that don't even exist in our color spectrum. As I looked down the center of this beautiful garden, I saw a large mountain with a waterfall flowing into a river of "living water." The river shined like crystals and bubbled like sparkling water. The river also had a light glowing from within it. As the water splashed, it also seemed to dance to the rhythm of the beautiful, musical tones.

I felt no pain or sorrow in this holy place. My body seemed weightless and filled with light, and I was so happy to be in paradise. Suddenly, out of the corner of my right eye, I caught a shimmer of light. I turned my face toward its direction and looked directly into the brightest light I had ever seen in my life. The light was pure white and extremely bright, yet I was able to look directly into it without shielding my eyes. As my eyes focused on this light, I began to see an outline of a man emerging from within the light. He was about one hundred yards away from me at the time. As the figure came into focus, I realized it was Jesus, and the bright light I saw was coming out of him.

Jesus stood waiting for me with his arms opened wide. I could feel the tears of joy welling up in my eyes, and I ran as fast as I could towards him. As I got closer, I could see Jesus' warm and beautiful smile radiating from his face. Like the prodigal son, I felt like a child who had been lost and found his way back home to his father. I ran into his open arms. As he embraced me, my body was engulfed in his light. I could feel his pure, unconditional love that poured out from within him. I stood there and bathed in his love. Jesus was tall and strong. Yet, he was gentle. Jesus looked like he was approximately thirty years old. However, his hair was silver and it also shined very bright. He had the most beautiful face I had ever seen.

I stood in his embrace with my head lying softly against his chest. I remember saying to him, "Lord Jesus, I've finally made it home." At first he didn't say a word, he just held me close. It was at this point that I recalled seeing the scars the nails had made on his hands and feet. Suddenly, I felt ashamed of all the sins he had borne for me. I mentally begged Jesus to forgive me of all the sins I had committed and for all the people I had hurt in my life and most of all for hurting him. Then Jesus did the most amazing thing that only a loving savior could do. Instead of judging or rebuking me for my sins, he began to pour out even more light and love into my wounded soul. I heard the words "peace be still" (KJV, Mark 4:39), and the storm that was raging inside of me was suddenly calmed just like the storm on the Sea of Galilee many years before.

Gently, he raised my face so I was able to look right into his eyes. Softly, he spoke to me and said, "No, my child, it is not your time. Your work is not complete." Never have I seen such love and compassion in any other eyes. I did not want to leave his loving embrace, but I knew I had to go. Instead of just releasing me, Jesus held me for a little while longer. Once again I felt the love pouring out from him, comforting and healing me. I realized he was giving me the strength for my journey back and for the work that he said was ahead of me. I will never forget the feeling of his embrace, and I long for the day when I will feel Jesus embrace me again. Finally, I looked into his eyes once more, and with a smile he gently released me.

As I walked away from him, I once again felt tears of joy welling up in my eyes. I kept looking back over my shoulder at Jesus for I did not want to take my eyes off him. I made my way back through the beautiful garden, gazing at its beauty one last time. I turned to look at Jesus once more and saw that he was still standing there smiling at me. Suddenly, I began to float up and over the wall of hedges. I landed back down onto the field of green grass with the tunnel in front of me. As I was about to enter the tunnel, I heard someone call my name. I turned and saw my great uncle Anthony Linquito standing there. I had been very close to him as a child. He passed away when I was 15 years old. I smiled and waved back at him. I guess he was there to guide me safely home. I remember going back down through the tunnel. Only this time there were no tormented souls in it. It was a peaceful journey.

When I woke up the next morning, I couldn't believe what had happened to me. Everything that had taken place felt so real. I asked myself, "Could this have been I dream?" Deep in my heart I knew it was not a dream. I somehow felt changed. I began to tremble, thinking, *Why would Jesus do this for me?* I felt so unworthy of this honor. *Why me, Lord, why me?*

Chapter Four

Blind, but Now I See

Over the next few weeks, I slowly began to feel his healing process. Jesus had set me free from the demons that had earlier clung to me. He released me from the anger, guilt, depression and shame that were such a big part of my life. I began to know what forgiveness meant. I learned not only to forgive, but to forgive and forget. For the first time I learned how to love all people through the eyes of Jesus, to love unconditionally no matter what their faults. For I had many! With just three simple words, "peace be still," suddenly it happened. The storm was gone and life was peaceful. As his disciples once said, "Who is this? Even the wind and the waves obey him!" (Mark 4:41).

I vowed never to tell anyone about my experience. I guess I was afraid that people would think I was crazy. In my mind I knew I wasn't crazy; however, I still wasn't quite sure what it all meant and where it would lead me. In time I would learn how

Jesus works.

Soon after this experience, I began my career as a professional musician. I was a singer for a show band that played in supper clubs around the tri-state area. We were becoming successful, and we had a large following. I was trying to move my life in a positive direction, but I still had a long way to go.

One evening a family came into one of the clubs at which we were appearing to celebrate their son John's twenty-first birthday. One of his sisters asked me if the band could play "Happy Birthday" while a waitress brought out a cake for her brother. After the band took a break, the young lady asked if we would like to have a piece of cake at their table. I went over to the table, said congratulations to John and had a piece of cake. The whole family told me how much they had enjoyed our show, and we all became friends. From that night on they began to follow our band faithfully.

I soon learned that John and I had many things in common. We were the same age and both into bodybuilding. We became workout partners at the gym. We also shared the same musical interests and passion for Harley Davidson motorcycles. We became close friends. However, at the time I didn't know John was a born-again Christian who was on fire for the Lord. One evening he slowly led me into a conversation about Jesus, and I began to pour out my soul. I told him everything, including my near-death experience, and to my surprise he believed me. We talked all night and what John had to say to me made sense. It was like someone turned the light bulb on. Suddenly, I began to clearly see who Jesus is. That night John gave me his personal Bible as a gift. I read it every day.

I soon began attending John's church on Sundays and Bible study class every Wednesday evening. I heard the testimonies of many people at these meetings, and most of the times their stories would reduce me to tears. Though the stories differed, they all had one thing in common. When they had finally asked Jesus into their hearts, their lives were changed forever. Now my life was changed forever.

I saw first hand what the power of Jesus could do. He had truly opened my eyes. I saw how other people overcame problems far worse than mine. I was filled with love and compassion for all of these people. I had finally found Jesus because now he dwelled in my heart. I realized it was Jesus who had led me to meet John and his family. Jesus had opened that door so that John could help me on the right path. Once he did, I never turned back. I am forever grateful to John for all he did for me. Thank you, Jesus, for opening that door. "I was blind but now I see!" (KJV, John 9:25).

Now with my faith confirmed, I was able to face the world once again. I got my life on track and was able to move forward. Gospel music became a big part of my life, and I began to write beautiful Christian songs. God had given me so many gifts and I finally began to use them.

Chapter Five

Angels Among Us

Do you believe in guardian angels? Well, I do, and his name was Eugene. Let me explain. One evening I got a telephone call from a gentleman with a thick Russian accent. He said his name was Eugene and that he worked with my mother. My mother had told him about my Christian music. Eugene was quite interested and had asked my mother if he could have my telephone number. Only a few minutes into our conversation, I could sense that Eugene was a kind and gentle soul, and there was something very special about him. We talked for a very long time about my music and my charity work. But mainly, we spoke about my relationship with Jesus. Before our conversation ended, Eugene invited me to his church and dinner at his home the following Sunday. I graciously accepted the invitation and hung up the phone. Somehow, I just knew that Eugene and I would become close friends.

Just as I predicted, Eugene and I did become close friends, and we shared many Sundays together visiting several local churches. Little by little, I realized just how many friends Eugene had in his life. He was loved by all who knew him. Each Sunday would always end with us sharing a delicious meal of Russian delicacies prepared lovingly by his wife. One Sunday afternoon while having coffee and dessert, Eugene told me his life story.

Eugene was a Russian immigrant who had served in the Russian army during WWII. He had been wounded several times and upon recovery had been sent back to the front lines. One day he had been captured by the Nazis and placed in a concentration camp. It was in the dead of winter and he had been given no clothing, food or shelter from the cold. The Nazis had been killing prisoners one by one. And to my horror, Eugene told me that he had been forced to sleep under dead bodies to keep warm. The atrocities of war that Eugene had endured were more than I could ever imagine. He stressed his hate for war and its senseless killings. His life had been spared because of his mechanical talents. He had been forced to repair German army vehicles for the Nazis. When the war ended, he had been released and went back to Russia. He never took one day for granted. At this time, Eugene's family had migrated to the United States.

Eugene and his family were very happy to live in a free country. Free to work, live and worship the way they wanted to. Every Sunday, Eugene would drive his mother-in-law to church. He would sit in the back of the church and wait to drive her home. One day while sitting in the back of the church, listening to the gospel, Eugene had opened his heart to Jesus Christ. From that point on, he never turned back. He lived the life Jesus would have wanted him to live. He was described by all who knew him as their Guardian Angel and that is exactly how I felt about him. He unselfishly gave of himself to anyone in need. He was always helping someone and never asked for anything in return.

One day when I was in Nashville, Tennessee, recording a gospel CD, my wife called and told me that Eugene was in the hospital. As soon as I returned, I went to see him. He was in intensive care and I was very concerned about him. I asked him what was wrong and if he was going to be alright. He told me that he was fine, although I knew better. He was more concerned about me and how my recording session had gone in Nashville. I played him the recording and he loved it!

By the end of the week, I drove him home from the hospital. He was frail, but I thought being discharged from the hospital was a good sign. A few days later I called to see how he was doing, and his daughter-in-law answered the telephone. She told me that Eugene had gone home to Jesus. I was shocked and devastated. But knowing Eugene's strong faith, he was exactly where he wanted to be. We had always planned to sing a duet together in Eugene's church. He wanted to sing his favorite song, "People Need the Lord." Unfortunately, this never came to be. However, I sing this song in tribute to him in my gospel concerts. Eugene was a big influence on me then and still is to this day. Meeting Eugene was no mistake. It was just another part of God's plan for me. Eugene was living proof that there are angels among us.

Chapter Six

The Confirmation

Being a performer, I have many people come up to me after a show and tell me how much they liked my voice and my performance, and it is always nice to hear such kind words. One day I was asked to sing at a church service in a nursing home. The home was filled with very old people, most in wheelchairs. After the gospel was read and the sermon was preached, I sang a few songs and ended the service with a song titled, "Look to Him." As I was singing, my heart was pouring out for all these people. Some of them were blind, others crippled and sick, yet they all sat there with smiles on their faces, smiling because they were happy hearing the Word of God. After I ended my song this very old woman reached her hand out to me. As I took her hand in mine she pulled me close and kissed me. With tears in her eyes she said, "Son, when you were singing I looked into your eyes, and I saw Jesus." I thanked her, and as tears welled up in my eyes, I kissed her gently on her cheek. Out of all the compliments I've received, those were the most beautiful words ever spoken to me. I will remember her kind words forever. Later I began to wonder if the old woman saw Jesus in my eyes because he now dwelled in my heart. Or was it his actual reflection that she saw because I had been graciously allowed to look upon his face several years earlier?

I was so thankful for the beautiful changes Jesus made in my life. It didn't seem to matter what the circumstances were for my redemption. I was grateful he had given me a second chance. What did matter was that I was living my life for Him.

Deep in my heart I still felt my vision of heaven and Jesus were real. However, in my mind I wasn't so sure. Had my soul really left my body or had it just been a beautiful dream? Over the next few years I would often ask myself this question.

During these years of spiritual growth and healing, I married my lovely wife, Jeannette. We had met in high school and dated for many years. She was in my life throughout all these events. She tried to help me when I was going through the bad times. I guess I had been too blind to realize this at the time. They say sometimes you hurt the one who loves you most. That was the case in my story, and I deeply regret this most of all. I am so sorry for all the pain I put her through. Luckily, for my sake, she saw something good in me and stuck by me until I saw the light, literally.

I continued to live my life for Jesus. I read my Bible faithfully and began to read religious and inspirational books. My library began to grow and still does today. One day I got the mail and there was a letter for a book-of-the-month club. I opened it and folded out a large sheet full of book titles. The page was filled with the actual book covers on little postage stamps. I looked at the books they had to offer and found one that caught my eye. I was in a rush, so I left the page on the counter in my kitchen. I forgot about the book club advertisement for a few days. When I finally remembered to look for it, the ad was gone. My wife, being the "neat freak" that she is, had thought it was junk mail and thrown it away. She said she was sorry and hadn't known that I was saving it. I said it didn't matter and that I would go to Barnes & Noble after dinner and look for the book. Shortly after dinner I left for the bookstore, and my quest began.

As I was driving I suddenly realized that I was going to look for a book without knowing the title or author. The only thing I had to go by was that I remembered the artwork on the cover. It was about 7:30 p.m. when I arrived at Barnes & Noble, and I began searching in the Religion/Christianity section. I had been searching for hours and was having no luck. I felt foolish asking the salesperson to help me due to the fact that I didn't have any information to give him. All at once I felt this strange feeling like I *had* to find this book and I had worked myself into a frenzy. I continued my search to no avail. At 10:45 p.m. the salesperson on the PA system asked all costumers to bring their selections to the sales counter.

At this point I was almost in tears, my body trembling from the anxiety of this unsuccessful search. I had searched every conceivable section in which this book might be and come up with nothing. I felt defeated, yet a voice inside my head was telling me to find this book. With nowhere to turn I began to make my way to the door. As I was about to exit the store, to my surprise I spotted the book. I recognized the book by the artwork on the cover. The title was *Embraced by the Light* by Betty Eadie. The book was a bestseller and they were featuring it on a book stand as you entered the store. Without realizing it I had passed by the book when entering the store. I began to laugh to myself, once again feeling foolish for spending so much time looking when it had been right in front of me all the time. I grabbed a copy of the book from the dozens on the stand and ran directly to the checkout.

Now the story comes full circle. When I got home from the

store that evening, I began reading the book. Once I started reading it, I couldn't put it down. I stayed up half the night until I finished reading it. When I closed the book, I realized why I was destined to find it. The book was a story about a woman who, after a major operation, had a near-death experience. I'd had no idea what the book was about before I read it. How could I? I hadn't even known the title or author of the book. The Lord certainly works in mysterious ways.

This story of the woman's out-of-body experience had so many similarities to mine. When her soul left her body, she went through the tunnel and into the light as I had. I know that is not an extraordinary statement because so many people who have had this experience make the same claim. Some of you may be thinking, okay, here's another nut with the tunnel and light story. Granted, if someone wanted to fabricate a near-death story that would be their first statement. Yet for me I find comfort in knowing that others who have truly had this experience have witnessed this same tunnel and light. It becomes a common bond for all who have been there. After Betty went through the tunnel and into the light, she arrived in paradise as I had. Here was where the story turned into a major revelation. Her description of heaven was so similar to mine it was as if I had written it myself. She described the flowers exactly the way I had seen them, light radiating from within. She talked about how every living thing had a musical tone to it and how the flowers and trees swayed to the music. She even described the mountain with its waterfall flowing into the river of living water. She spoke of Jesus and described him with shining silver hair like I had seen him.

The tears began to slowly fall as I was reading her account of heaven. Then all at once I lost it, and I began to cry uncontrollably. I realized the question I had been asking myself for years was finally answered. I now knew for sure that my near-death experience had not been just a dream; it had truly happened. The Lord had led me to this book to confirm what I had always thought deep in my heart was true. Looking back, there was no conceivable way I should have found that book under those circumstances. But through Jesus all things are possible.

Chapter Seven

Jesus Chose Me

Once again my life took a new turn. I was and still am able to face life with a different and beautiful outlook. I no longer have the fear of death and the unknown that plagues so many people. Jesus took away my fears and healed my wounded heart. I live my life for him every day. I don't know how I ever got through life without him. I guess it was like the poem "Footprints in the Sand." He carried me on his back through the bad times. Now my life is full, and I appreciate the little things it has to offer. I have learned to love unconditionally through the eyes of Jesus. I have seen the scars the nails left on his hands and feet, and I'm reminded each and every day what he did for me. Jesus paid the ransom for us all. He chose to bear our sins upon his shoulders and die for those sins by being nailed to a cross. The most amazing thing is that he left our sins at Calvary, and by his grace we are forgiven. He "Is" the Lamb of God who takes away all the sins of the world, and all he asks in return is that we believe in him! I remember hearing a line in a song that said, "The only manmade things in heaven are the scars on Jesus' hands." Now, I know that statement is true.

My music career also began to take off. I was signed to Lost Gold Records, an independent record company out of South Carolina in 1990. My single releases began to hit the top 10 and number 1 on the independent music charts. My music career was doing very well. I had won many awards and was inducted into the Alabama Country Music Hall of Fame.

One day Merle Kilgore, a big shot out in Nashville, called my producer and wanted to take over my contract and put me in the "Major Leagues." I felt as if all my prayers had been answered. I was signed to a major management contract by Merle Kilgore, who was the president of the Country Music Association and also managing Hank Williams Jr.

Merle brought me over to the McFadden agency, a production company that was one of the largest in Nashville, who then signed me on the spot. The McFaddens were handling Billy Ray Cyrus at the time, and he was riding high on the charts with a song called "Achy Breaky Heart." The owner, Jack, loved me and my music and saw superstardom in my future. I felt there was nothing that could stop me now. But God had a different plan for me.

The production company had put all the wheels in motion and said within 6 months everyone in the nation would know my name. Then suddenly everything came crashing down. My producer, Jack McFadden, died of a massive heart attack. Next, just as my first single was released, the major record label to which I was signed had to claim bankruptcy after 40 years in the business. They were stealing from their artists and weren't paying income tax. The IRS shut them down. I prayed, "Lord, please don't let this happen to me."

I pooled my resources and landed a job with Legends in Concert performing as Elvis in their shows. Once again all was going well. They were paying me a lot of money for doing something I really loved. Legends were so impressed with my road shows that they decided to offer me my own theater in Mesa Arizona as their "house" Elvis. This was in the summer of 2001. The new theater was going to open in January of 2002. Once again disaster struck in the form of 9/11. The entertainment industry was hit hard. No one felt like going out to see shows and I couldn't blame them. Legends began to lose major contracts with the casinos and cruise lines and never opened the new theater in Mesa.

I began to realize that I had been praying the wrong way for years. I was asking for things that I wanted to happen, not for God's will. I started to pray differently. I put my life in God's hands and asked Him to lead me wherever He wanted.

Soon after, my pastor asked me to sing as a soloist in my parish. Then a few months later he asked me to start a children's choir. Next, the principal of the school asked if I would be the leader of song for the Monday morning school liturgies. I couldn't believe how fast things were happening. If that wasn't enough, the principal informed me that they no longer had a music teacher and asked me if I would fill the position. I accepted, and before I knew it, two other Catholic school principals asked me to teach music at their schools. I now had a full-time job teaching music to children and loving it. I realized that what I had been searching for all over the country had been in my own backyard all the time. I had finally "made it big." No, I'm not a household name; I've made it bigger than that. Jesus chose me for ministry!

Currently, my music career has also taken a positive turn. I am busier than ever with Elvis tribute shows, country music shows and Christian music shows. I continue to tour the country in the summer doing outdoor concerts and festivals to large audiences. During the school year while I'm teaching, I perform at local concerts and various charity events. I continue to write and record country and Christian music and have several CD releases to my credits.

Chapter Eight

Forever Grateful

I don't know why Jesus allowed me this beautiful glimpse of heaven. I have never felt worthy of it, yet I am forever grateful. When he sent me back he said that my work was not complete. I still don't know exactly what he has planned for me. Maybe it's to share my story of heaven with those who have lost all hope like I once did. I am no longer afraid to share this story and worry what people might think. I will share this story with all who care to hear it and even with ones who don't. Or maybe it's the musical gifts he has given me. When I sing in church and see the faces in the congregation in tears, I know that my song is blessed by the power of the Holy Spirit. I know it is not me who moves them. It is Jesus using me as a vessel to spread his love, hope and compassion. If I helped save just one soul, then my life has been worthwhile. Jesus died for us all, but he loves us so much that he would have died for only one. Whatever he wants of me, I am willing to give for he gave his life for me. Now I know what he meant when he said, "I am with you always" (KJV, Matthew 28:20). He walks beside me, and his voice guides me through each and every day of my life.

There are so many extraordinary stories I could share with you and maybe one day I will write them all. As this chapter in my life comes to an end, I have to say that I've been truly blessed. God has given me my beautiful wife, Jeannette, and two wonderful sons, Christian and Joshua. We are a happy and loving Christian family. I try my best to instill the words that Jesus taught us in my sons. He said to " Love one another as I have loved you" (KJV, John 13:34). I love my family more than words can say. Thank you, Lord.

As this story comes to a close, I pray that Jesus will continue to bless me with the strength, love and guidance to follow the path he has chosen for me. For many years I have felt the calling to spread the gospel through an outreach ministry that will help those in need. If it is God's will, I hope to become a deacon in the Catholic Church. I pray that once I complete my studies and I'm ordained as a deacon, Jesus will once again strengthen and guide me for this next exciting chapter in my life.

Epilogue

I would like to leave you with the lyrics to one of my songs, titled "On the Third Day."

On the Third Day

(Lyrics and music by Anthony Liguori, Jr. and Joseph Durante)

Jesus said, "Destroy this temple, three days I'll raise it up again"
They thought for sure this time, he'd really lost his mind
But He changed water into wine
You see the temple that he spoke of wasn't one made out of stone.
It was flesh and bone
They nailed him to the cross
The King had paid the cost for you and me
But on the third day just like He said He would
On the third day, they didn't think He really could
The prophecy was filled, it was what the Father willed

The King could not be stilled
On the third day, on the third day
So raise every heart with Jesus, every knee bend to His name
He will come again, his glory to behold
And it's still the greatest story ever told
'Cause on the third day, like he said he would
On the third day, they didn't think he really could
The victory was won, He is the Father's Son
Oh death where is thy sting, you can hear the angels sing
Glory to the newborn King, on the third day.
On the third day.

Printed in the United States
49064LVS00005B/15